Snakes on the Hunt

# SEA SNAKES

Gale George

**PowerKiDS**
press

New York

Published in 2017 by The Rosen Publishing Group, Inc.
29 East 21st Street, New York, NY 10010

First Edition

Editor: Caitie McAneney
Book Design: Mickey Harmon

Photo Credits: Cover, pp. 1, 4, 6, 8, 14, 16, 18, 20 (series logo) iLoveCoffeeDesign/Shutterstock.com; cover, pp. 1, 3, 4, 6, 8, 10, 12, 14, 16, 18, 20, 22—24 (background) cla78/Shutterstock.com; cover (sea snake), pp. 5, 19 Rich Carey/Shutterstock.com, p. 7 (inset) Jason Edwards/National Geographic/Getty Images; p. 7 (main) Michael & Patricia Fogden/Minden Pictures/Getty Images; p. 9 Ethan Daniels/Shutterstock.com; p. 11 ullstein bild/Contributor/ullstein bild/Getty Images; p. 13 Paul Sutherland/National Geographic/Getty Images; p. 15 tae208/Shutterstock.com; p. 17 Auscape/Contributor/Universal Images Group Editorial/Getty Images; p. 21 https://commons.wikimedia.org/wiki/File:Pelamis_Platurus_Costa_Rica.JPG; p. 22 paul cowell/Shutterstock.com.

Cataloging-in-Publication Data

Names: George, Gale.
Title: Sea snakes / Gale George. 689 0860
Description: New York : PowerKids Press, 2017. | Series: Snakes on the hunt | Includes index.
Identifiers: ISBN 9781499422061 (pbk.) | ISBN 9781499422085 (library bound) | ISBN 9781499422078 (6 pack)
Subjects: LCSH: Sea snakes–Juvenile literature.
Classification: LCC QL666.O64 G44 2017 | DDC 597.96'5–d23

Manufactured in the United States of America

CPSIA Compliance Information: Batch #BS16PK: For Further Information contact Rosen Publishing, New York, New York at 1-800-237-9932

# Contents

# Snakes in the Sea

What could be scarier than snakes on dry land? How about snakes in the water? You may be surprised to learn that the world's most **venomous** snakes live underwater.

There are more than 60 different species, or kinds, of sea snakes. They're part of the cobra family. They use their venom when hunting eels, fish, mollusks, and **crustaceans**. Lucky for us, they're generally calm, and attacks on people are rare. Would you be afraid to see a snake underwater?

## Snake Bites

The banded sea krait has some of the strongest venom in the world.

All snakes can swim, but sea snakes live in the water.

# Made for the Water

Sea snakes are usually 3 to 5 feet (0.9 to 1.5 m) long, but some are much longer. They've **adapted** to life in the water. Their tail is flattened like a paddle, which helps them swim. The openings of their nose can seal shut to keep water out. Sea snakes have special body parts that help remove extra salt from their body.

Sometimes people see a sea snake and think it's an eel. Eels are able to breathe underwater, but sea snakes have a **lung** and must surface for air.

## Snake Bites

Small, flattened heads help sea snakes move quickly through the water. Yellow-bellied sea snakes can dive at speeds faster than 3 feet (0.9 m) per second when they're hunting or need to swim away.

This is a yellow-bellied sea snake. Sea snakes come in many colors and patterns.

# Baby Sea Snakes

True sea snakes don't lay eggs. Instead, eggs grow and hatch inside the mother's body. Mothers can give birth to 20 live young. The size of babies is different by species. Yellow-bellied sea snakes are born about 10 inches (25.4 cm) long.

Sea kraits leave the water to find a **mate** and lay their eggs on the shore. That makes them amphibious. Amphibious snakes aren't true sea snakes. They live both in the water and on land.

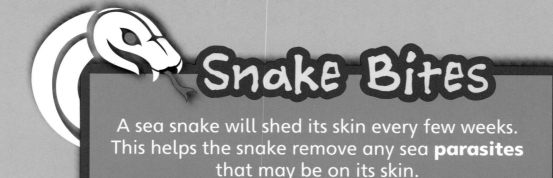

## Snake Bites

A sea snake will shed its skin every few weeks. This helps the snake remove any sea **parasites** that may be on its skin.

Many people consider the banded sea krait to be a sea snake because it spends most of its time in the water. However, it's not a true sea snake because it sometimes goes to shore. This one is spending time on an island during mating season.

# Life at Sea

Sea snakes mostly live in the warm waters of the Pacific Ocean and Indian Ocean. They live in **estuaries**, **coral reefs**, the open ocean, and other places. About half of all sea snake species are found off the coast of western Australia.

The yellow-bellied sea snake has the largest range of all snake species. They can be found from the eastern coast of Africa to Australia and Japan. Ocean currents can carry them as far as the western shores of Central America!

yellow-bellied sea snake area

A banded sea krait searches for a meal in its coral home.

## Snake Bites

Most snakes like to live alone, but sea snakes are sometimes seen together in groups.

# Sea Snake Senses

Like other snakes, sea snakes flick out their tongue to smell. Their tongue passes the smells to the Jacobson's **organ**, which identifies them. This is how sea snakes investigate, or learn about, their surroundings.

Most sea snakes are able to breathe through their skin! This means they can stay underwater longer. They also have a long lung that helps them store air. Sea snakes can dive several hundred feet into the ocean and stay underwater for up to two hours.

Sea snakes are active during the day and at night. This is an olive sea snake.

# Very Venomous

Sea snakes have short, pointed teeth called fangs that they use for hunting **prey**. They won't usually attack other creatures unless they're bothered by predators, such as eels, sharks, and eagles. Some sea snakes are brightly colored, which warns predators to stay away.

One of the most venomous sea snakes is the Belcher's sea snake. Just a small amount of its venom could kill hundreds of people. Luckily, this snake tends to avoid humans, and only about one in four of its bites has venom in it.

## Snake Bites

Sea snakes may use their flattened tails to trick predators into thinking that they have two heads. Predators may attack the snake's tail, which keeps its head safe.

Sea kraits poke around in coral looking for prey, which leaves them unaware of their surroundings and makes them easier to attack.

# What's for Dinner?

Sea snakes are carnivores, which means they eat only meat. They love to eat fish, crustaceans, eels, and mollusks. They also eat the eggs of other sea creatures that they find while hunting around rocks and reefs. Some kinds of sea snake will eat only certain types of fish.

Like other types of snakes, sea snakes can open their jaws wide so they can eat bigger prey. Sometimes they eat fish that are two or three times bigger than the size of their neck!

## Snake Bites

Yellow-bellied sea snakes drink fresh rainwater that pools on the surface of the ocean. They can go for half a year between drinks!

This fish is the perfect size for a sea snake snack!

# On the Hunt!

When hunting, sea snakes search around in coral and rocks for prey. They feel vibrations, or small movements, in the water when a fish swims near. That helps them hunt in the dark. Then it's time to strike!

Sea snakes have short fangs, but their venom is very toxic and works quickly to bring down prey. They mostly use their venom for hunting, not for **defense**. Venom also helps sea snakes **digest** their food by breaking down their prey's flesh before they even eat it.

## Snake Bites

Yellow-bellied sea snakes will sometimes float motionless at the surface, waiting to surprise their prey. When a curious fish swims up from below, the snake will quickly snap it up.

This sea krait is searching the coral for its next meal.

19

# Snakes in Danger

Sea snakes have few natural predators. Many predators realize sea snakes are venomous, so they won't attack. People are often a bigger danger. Sea snakes can get tangled in fishing lines or nets. Some are hit by boats.

Another problem for true sea snakes is ending up on land. Sometimes they're washed ashore or dropped on land by a bird. It's very hard for true sea snakes to move on land, and they often die.

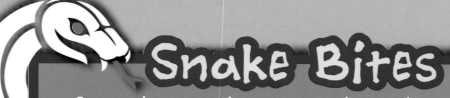

## Snake Bites

Sea snakes sometimes approach people out of curiosity, but they don't want to hurt them. Most bites happen when fishermen catch sea snakes in their nets.

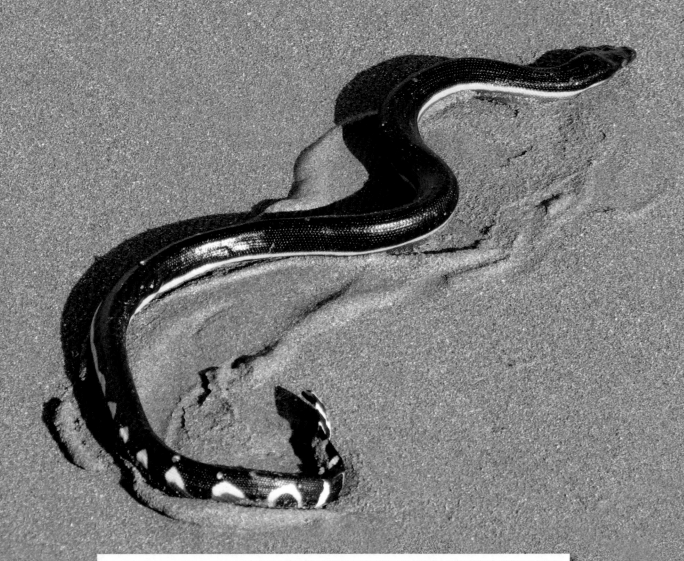

Storms and fast currents also move sea snakes out of their natural **habitats**. They can end up on land or in waters that are too cold for them to survive.

# Protecting Sea Snakes

In late 2015 and early 2016, several yellow-bellied sea snakes washed ashore in Southern California, well north of their normal territory. This is likely because warmer than usual temperatures caused warmer waters. Sea snakes, like many other ocean animals, are at risk of losing their natural habitats.

How can you help? Let people know about these amazing sea creatures and their habitats. And if you see a sea snake, let it swim away safely. It's only hunting!

# Glossary

**adapt:** To change to suit conditions.

**coral reef:** The hard remains of coral animals that form a line in ocean waters.

**crustacean:** An animal with a hard shell, jointed limbs, feelers, and no backbone.

**defense:** A feature of a living thing that helps keep it safe.

**digest:** To break down food inside the body so that the body can use it.

**estuary:** An area where the ocean's tide meets a river.

**habitat:** The natural place where an animal or plant lives.

**lung:** A part of an animal that takes in air when it breathes.

**mate:** One of two animals that come together to produce babies.

**organ:** A body part that does a certain task.

**parasite:** A living thing that lives in, on, or with another living thing and often harms it.

**prey:** An animal hunted by other animals for food.

**venomous:** Having a poisonous bite or sting.

# Index

# Websites

Due to the changing nature of Internet links, PowerKids Press has developed an online list of websites related to the subject of this book. This site is updated regularly. Please use this link to access the list: www.powerkidslinks.com/soth/seas